Tiggy Bayley

Squidge

Salamander Street

PLAYS

First published in 2026 by Salamander Street Ltd., a Wordville imprint. (info@salamanderstreet.com).

Cover photograph by Amy Lauffer

Playwright's headshot by Yuqian Shi

Interior photography from rehearsals by Ciaran Wilson

ISBN: 9781919483252

10 9 8 7 6 5 4 3 2 1

Further copies of this publication can be purchased from www.salamanderstreet.com

FOREWORD

Tiggy and I first set eyes on each other while training on the StoneCrabs Directors In Practice Programme. We were always the first ones to volunteer to do the acting and improvisation exercises. Here I discovered Tiggy's genius as both a writer and a performer—her dry humour that catches you off-guard, her pokes at the absurdity of life, her constant search for the beauty in people. Little did I know, at that time, she was pouring her heart into her first play, *Squidge*.

Tiggy sent me an early draft of *Squidge* during a quiet shift at my day job. When I read the first line "Fat Lump", I knew I was reading something special so I locked myself in the stock cupboard and read it in one sitting. I left the cupboard with that feeling all directors know but don't get often, a mixture of butterflies, giddiness and awe right at the bottom of my belly. I thought: "Tiggy's got to do this, and I've got to direct it." Tiggy and I met at a Vietnamese restaurant in Islington and I tried to play it cool, but at the end of our chat I just blurted it out: "I really want to direct it and I think I'd be really good at it." Tiggy was just as forthcoming: "I want to take it to Edinburgh Fringe this summer"—it was June at the time.

We didn't take it to the fringe that year, so we had over a year to take our time and develop it slowly. Tiggy had to perform the play herself; the script was written in her voice and it fit her natural comic timing. This led to a joyful actor-writer creative process where, instead of having stale script meetings between drafts then rehearsals, we could explore the play, ask questions, make edits, block and rehearse in tandem, on our feet, in a rehearsal room. By the time the next Edinburgh Fringe came along, it was perfectly formed.

Squidge is a sign of our times and puts a mirror to the dire state of the UK today; the disparity of wealth, the mental health epidemic and our underfunded education system. These are all issues we know and experience every day and sometimes they can feel too big and systemic to have any impact. *Squidge* tells us that we can change the world in little ways, in our little lives, if we just choose love and bring it into everything we do.

Squidge is also timeless; the message about choosing love in dark times continues to be relevant, the jokes have never dried up and the human experience of grief can never be cured. We might not all have worked in a school, lost a loved one to addiction or had sex with our plumber, but we have all experienced life and the darkness, loss and love it brings.

So I hope you can find a quiet stock cupboard, lock yourself inside, read the play in one sitting and come out with butterflies in your belly.

Selwin Hulme-Teague

2026

WRITER'S NOTE

My perspective on the world is that it is a cruel place but that there is beauty in pain. The connections we make with each other are the most important things that we have. That is at the heart of *Squidge*. The worst moments in my life have not been defined by the bad and the ugly, but by the good, by the moments of kindness and generosity of good people who have helped to pull me out of the darkness and into the light. *Squidge* carries a hopeful message in ways that are nuanced, funny and emotionally powerful. In writing this play I wanted to draw attention to the good in the world. It was about taking a stand against people who do the wrong thing and showing that every one of us, like Daisy, has a chance to do the right thing, to do good in the everyday.

Squidge is derived from years of working in inner-city schools and witnessing where children in poverty fit into the system (between the cracks at the bottom). The idea for Daisy as a character first came in 2020 in the form of a sketch. Then I crafted her, listened to her and shaped her into a real, grief-stricken young woman trying to find her place in the world. I wrote the play during a very difficult time in my life. Showing up for the kids and going into school helped to get me through it. I think the best way of helping yourself is sometimes helping other people.

I tend to write from the soul first. I note down bits of inspiration and things that excite me on post-it notes. Like snippets of astonishingly boring conversation in the staffroom or moments of ridicule from the fire drill. I start to flesh those out and imagine characters, often drawing on real life experiences. Then I arrange them into a structure, a bit like they do in detective shows, thinking about what fits where. I know other writers who start with structure but I don't do that. I've found there's no right way to do it, it's been about finding what works for me and building it into a daily routine.

Before I found the show's title, it was going to be called *Looking for Angels* or something equally naff. I decided to name it *Squidge* in rehearsal as Selwin questioned its significance. I realised that *Squidge* represents hope or the belief that life will get better. I'm forever grateful for the collaborative nature of White Noise Theatre that champions actor-writers and was forever encouraging me to enhance the script, and grateful to Selwin for not always agreeing with me but always believing in me.

I've now written the pilot for *Squidge* as a TV series, and for the national tour we added in a couple of bits from that, notably the lizard jokes, a little more car fetish and the yoga scene with Mum. At its heart *Squidge* has always been a story about Daisy and Paddy. A redemptive platonic love story, an emotional roller coaster, a cathartic journey with a degree of you-can't-cry-if-you're-laughing which, I hope, makes it easier to enjoy and therefore more powerful.

Tiggy Bayley
2026

THANK YOU

Firstly, to Selwin. My director, friend and confidant. Your heart, dedication and precision know no bounds. What a joy it is to have had you on this journey for the last two years, growing and learning together in the spirit of optimism that is *Squidge*.

Thank you to all those who gave me feedback in the early stages. To Mum who proofreads every draft and every boring-ass funding application that I write. To my sister, Clara, who encourages me even when nothing in the world makes sense. And to Lena Vurma, my all-time favourite hype-woman.

To the wonderful producers who have helped get this show out there, Linda-Ray Ndlovu, Izzy Parriss and Poppy Maxwell.

Thank you to the venues that have given us a platform to do so: The Cockpit, Burning Coal Theatre, Sweet Action Theatre, Theatre503, Interplay Theatre, Chapel Barn, Exeter Phoenix, Seven Dials Playhouse, Pleasance Courtyard / Edinburgh Fringe Festival, Soho Theatre, Theatre@41, Wardrobe Theatre, Yvonne Arnaud Theatre, Riverside Studios. Thank you to The Offies and The Popcorn Award for your recognition.

Thanks to Soho Theatre for having me on their stage and to Lee Griffiths in particular and everyone else in the Edinburg Lab who made me laugh and gave me kindness and a community through the whirlwind that was Fringe.

And the Arts Council for giving us a grant to develop the show.

My acting coach Mr. Laurence Mitchell. For all his advice, friendship and for the knowledge that I already have everything I need.

Mark Mills for telling me to stay fighting when the chips were down.

Luke Barnes who encourages me to remind myself that I am an artist every day, even when I'm working a day job in a uniform that says something else.

My agent, Mia, who believed in me when it felt like no one else did. And to Rosie and Ava at PFD, I'm so looking forward to the road ahead.

Thank you to all the female solo playwrights whose books are on my bookshelf encouraging me to write down my perspective on the world.

My friends, my wonderful friends that have stuck by me through thick and thin, "when faith is gone let it be borrowed". Thank you to my friends for their unwavering support.

And, of course, to my very dear, very dysfunctional family who have sat through this show too many times. Ben, Clara, Susan and Mum and Dad. I love you.

And lastly, to the lost souls I have taught along the way. You served as the inspiration for this play. You taught me more than you know.

Squidge was first performed at Theatre503 on 8th March 2024. It was then performed at Pleasance on 31stJuly 2024 as part of the Edinburgh Fringe Festival. It transferred to Soho Theatre, London on 20th February 2025 and Riverside Studios, London on 24th March 2026. The cast were as follows:

DAISY	**Tiggy Bayley**
Writer	**Tiggy Bayley**
Director and Dramaturg	**Selwin Hulme-Teague**
Producer	**White Noise Theatre**
Production Manager	**Linda-Ray Ndlovu**
Lighting Designer	**Amelia Fenwick**
Stage Manager and Operator	**Luke Madzudzo**
Cinematographer	**Benjamin Leggett**
Promotion Photography	**Reece McCullagh & Ciaran Wilson**
Acting Coach	**Laurence Mitchell**
Voice Coach	**Adam Rhys-Charles**
Voice Coach Assistant	**Mol Jo Tucker**

CREATIVE TEAM

Tiggy Bayley | Writer & Performer

Tiggy is a writer and performer with a degree in Liberal Arts. Her last three short films received multiple awards for both performance and screenwriting and have been screened at BIFA-qualifying festivals including the British Urban Film Festival and Brighton Rocks Film Festival. She was shortlisted for Film London's Lodestars 2023 and selected for BAFTA Connect. Her debut feature *Tildypops* was selected for development by Torino Film Lab Next Comedy, and is currently in financing. Tiggy won the Goldfinch Writer's Award 2024 for her project, *The Fat Queen*. She is currently writing her second feature, a psychological horror.

Tiggy trained in theatre at Jacques Lecoq in Paris, and has directed work at venues including The Cockpit and Southwark Playhouse. Her debut one-woman show *Squidge* was shortlisted for the BBC Popcorn Writing Award at the Edinburgh Fringe and went on to a sold-out run at Soho Theatre in London in 2025 followed by a national tour.

Tiggy recently filmed a role in BBC's *Strike*. She lives in South London with Larry, her cat, and loves cooking.

Selwin Hulme-Teague | Director

Selwin is Artistic Director of White Noise Theatre. He studied English and Theatre at the University of Warwick and trained in directing with StoneCrabs Directors in Practice Programme and Young Vic Fresh Direction.

Theatre: *Squidge* (Theatre503, Interplay Theatre, Chapel Barn, Exeter Phoenix, Seven Dials Playhouse, Pleasance Courtyard / Edinburgh Fringe Festival, Soho Theatre, Theatre@41, Wardrobe Theatre, Yvonne Arnaud Theatre, Riverside Studios), *Wakey Wakey!* (Discover Children's Story Centre, Newham Festival of Stories), *Champagne* (Old Red Lion Theatre), *Sirena* (The Glitch), *Back to the Moon* (The Glitch), *Joe Carstairs* (Omnibus Theatre, Quay Arts), *NewsRevue* (Canal Cafe Theatre), *My Dad Wears*

A Dress (Vagina Museum, Nottingham Playhouse, Greenwich Theatre, The PEN Theatre, FUSE Festival, Edinburgh Fringe Festival), *PlantGays* (Exeter Phoenix, The Greenhouse Theatre, Omnibus Theatre, Chapel Barn), *The Black Cat* (King's Head Theatre, Omnibus Theatre), *I Kermit* (Lion & Unicorn Theatre) and *The Pizza Inspector* (Schools tour).

Workshop: *The Well of Loneliness* (Omnibus Theatre), *Bear* (Wilton's Music Hall), *Untitled Sex Health Show* (Vagina Museum, Exeter Phoenix, Chapel Barn, Playhouse East), *COARSE* (Camden People's Theatre), *Selkie* (National Theatre Scotland), *[redacted due to budgetary constraints]* and the *Kingdom of Crystal's Skull* (Leicester Curve) and *HEDDA* (Farnham Maltings)

With Drama Schools: *A Musical Parody Show* (Liverpool Institute of Performing Arts), *Tartuffe* (Rose Bruford College) and *Eliza and the Purple Monster* (British Youth Music Theatre)

As Assistant Director: *Caligari* (New Diorama, Edinburgh Fringe Festival), *these words that'll linger like ghosts until the day i drop down dead* (Riverside Studios), *Peter Pan* (Powderham Castle), *Tethered* (Lion & Unicorn Theatre), *Fires Our Shoes Have Made* (Edinburgh Fringe Festival) and *Macbeth* (Barbican Theatre Plymouth).

White Noise Theatre | Producer

White Noise Theatre creates collaborative new writing with actor-writers, leading to a unique style of work that combines the rawness of verbatim with the craft of fiction.

The company was co-founded by Selwin Hulme-Teague and Rebecca James at the University of Warwick. Their first show *Potatoes* was selected for the National Student Drama Festival in 2020. Subsequent shows include: *PlantGays* (Omnibus Theatre, The Greenhouse Theatre, Chapel Barn and Exeter Phoenix), *Untitled Sex Health Show* (Chapel Barn, Exeter Phoenix, Vagina Museum, Playhouse East), *Squidge* (Theatre503, Interplay Theatre, Chapel Barn, Exeter Phoenix, Seven Dials Playhouse, Pleasance Courtyard / Edinburgh Fringe Festival, Soho Theatre, Theatre@41, Wardrobe Theatre, Yvonne Arnaud Theatre, Riverside Studios). They also host an annual scratchnight and development programme for actor-writers called *Write Noise Night*.

WITH SUPPORT FROM:

For all the lonely people

Tiggy Bayley

Squidge

CHARACTERS

DAISY
Early twenties

NOTES ON THE PLAY

The original play was done with a chair, a raincoat and a mobile phone. The raincoat was used to define the space in which Daisy found herself, by wearing it, hanging it up at school and putting it on the floor at home. The set and props should be at the director's discretion.

DAISY sits on a red school chair.

DAISY: Fat lump. I can see him waddling down the corridor through the rectangular window in the classroom door. 45 minutes late. The rest of them, knee-deep in fractions, already done their spellings.

He opens the door. Doesn't even have a school bag.

Uniform's a shambles, jumper too tight, black trainers non-regulation. Maybe we'll get on.

He slumps in. Fat lump. And he's looking at me, I can tell what he's thinking—why are you sat in my seat? Cause I am.

I've been sat here in your little kiddie chair for 45 mins tidying your desk, sharpening your pencils and waiting for you to arrive.

And here you are.

He turns to the classroom teacher, Mr Murray. Irish cunt and asks, who's this?

Murray answers for me. He's like a small, Irish pelican. A pelican because he's got a really big, protruding chin.

MR MURRAY: This, Paddy, is your new wee helper. Miss Wright.

DAISY: He turns on his heels and walks straight back out the door. Fine by me. Do you think I want to be here? I'm not a teacher. I don't want to be a teacher. I hate everyone. Especially children. I'm only here because Recruitment Paul wouldn't stop calling me. And I've run out of savings. And apparently, I need to do something besides lying in bed all day eating Rice Krispies.

Pelican's looking at me. Expectantly.

Oh, he wants me to follow him. Fuck's sake.

DAISY gets up, storms out of the room to follow PADDY.

We spend the rest of the day in the learning support room. Paddy tells me about his family. It's a big family, he's got five siblings, no four. Then he looks sad... He's the eldest so that comes with a lot of responsibility because he's Irish.

I already know he's a traveller from his file. An Irish traveller. He's Irish. He tells me he's Irish about five times.

He can count to five in Irish: one, two, tree, four, five.

(Sarcastically, to PADDY) Impressive.

We start looking at animal books. He's obsessed with snakes. He says he wants to be a vet when he's older. Don't tell him that he might need to be able to read first.

He's ten but his reading age is that of a six-year-old. He tells me that he hates school. He's hated it since year three when Ms Grimsby sat him at the back of the class with the desk facing the back wall. Gave him fidget spinners to fiddle with.

MS GRIMSBY: *(nasal voice)* Paddy, if you're not going to participate with the rest of the class you'll need to stay at the back.

DAISY: I've seen her around school, dresses like Pippy Longstocking with odd socks and pigtails just to be controversial. It's annoying.

Paddy's in Mr Murray's class now because they're hoping he might be able to use the Irish thing to get him back into learning. And me.

He tells me about his pet lizard and shoplifting with his mum. I wonder if that's a safeguarding issue? Decide it's not.

I'm not a teacher and I'm not responsible for anyone. I only got this job because Mr Murray made me laugh in the interview and I have a smile that lights up the room. I may look sweet, but my insides are odious.

I tell Paddy how to spell snake.

Look up lizard jokes on his tablet. I get some coloured paper and we draw his name in snake letters. Except he spells his last name wrong.

I don't tell him.

I get home and sink into my sofa. I'm not lonely but I am alone. Sometimes I go for walks. Midnight walks. Take Arthur's coat.

I don't really see my friends, they're all busy with their partners and they don't remember that I exist. Some of them came to the funeral which was nice. Gave me flowers.

They're on my coffee table. Tulips and lilies and chrysanthemums. They're all dead now which is ironic. But it means I can see the TV again.

My phone rings. Mum. No one else calls me. I pretend I'm not going to answer but I do. I always do.

MUM: Hi darling.

DAISY: Since Arthur died, every time she calls me she says, "Hi darling" and then nothing. And I don't say anything. I don't have anything to say.

MUM: Daisy? Are you doing okay?

DAISY: *(to MUM)* Yeah, good. You?

And then she says something irrelevant like…

MUM: This world wasn't easy for him. He'll be happier where he is now.

DAISY: I hang up. Not because I'm trying to be rude but because these calls do nothing for me.

I text the plumber. He came to fix a leak a couple of weeks ago. The day after the funeral. We fucked. It was great so we're still fucking. He's a single dad and I think the sex is good because it's mixed up with grief. It's like we both know what deep sadness is, so we don't have to talk about it.

We can just fuck and pretend it doesn't exist. Communicate through the sadness in our eyes. Without words.

I hate talking. But sometimes when we're having sex it feels like I have someone to talk to.

He says he can't talk right now because it's his kid's birthday. So I say, "OK Daddy." And he doesn't reply so I have a wank and fall asleep on my sofa.

—

Sofa. Wanking. Walking. Sofa. Wanking. School.

DAISY puts on a raincoat.

I arrive late because it's raining and you can clean out my cunt and fuck me sideways if you think I'm leaving any earlier just because it's raining. I arrive soaking. It's a 12-minute walk from my car because there's nowhere to park in the deepest darkest arse-end of Sydenham.

MR MURRAY: The kids are in P.E.

DAISY: *(to MR MURRAY)* Oh, nice.

DAISY goes to take off her raincoat.

MR MURRAY: You have to supervise P.E.

DAISY: He looks annoyed at me, like I've already taken up too much of his energy by arriving. I look out of the window at the playground. They're all running round in little yellow bibs like minions. Little yellow minions—there's Paddy!

(to MR MURRAY) Can I not supervise from up here?

MR MURRAY: I don't think so.

DAISY: Next thing I know, I'm sat on a picnic bench in the prison yard that they call a playground. The kids are running round screaming with bibs hanging out their arses like tails—it's part of the game, they have to try and steal each other's tails…

I've got my phone under the table. Sexting the plumber. "Do you have any rope in that van of yours?"

"I want you to tie me up."

"Cum in my mouth."

"Slide your finger into my…"

MR MURRAY: Daisy? Daisy?!

DAISY: Phone away. Sheepish. Like one of the kids.

MR MURRAY: Daisy, you need to watch Paddy. He's being inappropriate. I can see him being inappropriate from the window.

DAISY: See. I told you I could supervise from the window… I look up, about to tell him it's all under control but then I see Paddy chasing this girl. And he's got his bib in the air, trying to whack her arse with it.

Fuck's sake.

(to PADDY) Paddy. Paddy Connors.

I wish his name didn't sound like a country singer from the 90s, it makes it hard to get angry.

(to PADDY) Mr Connors. Come with me NOW.

I grab him by the hand and drag him inside. He's pulling on me. Heels digging into the floor.

I get him to the bottom of the stairwell, the spine that goes up the centre of the school. And his knees give way and he lies down—face down—spread out like one of those dead animal rugs.

In the middle of the fucking school.

I bend down so my face is just above his. He looks up at me through red demon eyes. Venom spews from his mouth like a snake.

(to PADDY) You are not going back outside.

He makes a run for it, tries to leap up off the floor but I see it coming. No chance. Tackle him back to the ground.

(to PADDY) Paddy Connors. Stop misbehaving. You were messing around in P.E. and now you have to face the consequences. Whatever Squidge is, you're not getting it. Sit down. I've seen Mr Murray talk like that with his beak.

I push on Paddy's shoulders, force him back to the floor.

(to PADDY) Thank you.

We sit cross-legged, opposite each other. There's a long pause.

And then he erupts. Tears start pouring from every crevice of his fat face.

Then these whale noises.

DAISY does the whale noises.

He says, "It's my fault. I didn't mean for him to die. It's all my fault."

I don't know what he's talking about. The only things on his Special Needs report were "Irish traveller", "snakes" and "motor difficulties" so I know he finds it hard to hold a pen…

He's literally sobbing. Crying, "I just want someone to bring him back."

But kids are weird and they'll do anything to get out of trouble.

I don't know what to do so I do nothing. I just sit there while he sobs.

Five minutes.

Ten minutes.

20 minutes.

The class come back inside, traipse past us, up the stairs.

55 minutes. Until he finally. Stops crying. I'm not paid enough for this.

(to PADDY) What do you want to do now?

He shrugs. Rude.

(to Paddy) Okay. I'll tell you what I want. I want to go back to class and make this fu-- miserable day a little bit less miserable by pretending nothing happened. Maybe read about some snakes.

Paddy, why did the lizard break up with his girlfriend?

He looks up at me. Fat, swollen tear-stained face and says, "because she waS tOo ClingY" and we make it up the stairs.

A few weeks in, I'm asked to attend school early on Mondays to help the SENCO, that's the Special Educational Needs Coordinator, in running a morning session for the kids with Special Educational Needs.

(in SENCO's voice) She's got this really light patronising voice that sounds like she's been abused at Christian camp for years.

She thinks that getting them all together once a week helps set them up with a healthy attitude to learning.

I think it serves as a hotbed for radicalisation where they'll learn the worst and most annoying behaviours they can from each other.

I ask if I'll get paid more to come in early. No reply.

This Monday is particularly fun. She starts by introducing us all to Squidge.

DAISY pretends to be SENCO, miming squidging air into an imaginary ball and placing it on top of her head.

SENCO: Meet Squidge. For those of you who haven't met him, he's an imaginary ball of brain juice and boogers and imagination. Now, Squidge will sit on top of my head and watch today's session. At the end of today's session, Squidge will be given to someone, anyone, who's behaved really, really well. And if you're lucky enough to get Squidge, you can colour him any colour you want.

DAISY: She pulls down a poster of three emojis: a green smiley faced emoji, an amber straight-faced emoji and an angry red-faced emoji and asks the children to point at the emoji which best describes how they're feeling this morning.

There's Ryan (ADHD and anger management) on red, Yusuf (autistic) on green, Gemma (ADD and violent) on orange, Tobi (learning difficulties) on green and Paddy on red.

It's a party.

SENCO: We will get to play football for ten minutes at the end of the session provided everyone listens well to instructions and focuses on getting to the green zone, ready to start the day of learning.

DAISY: The following exercise is simple, we take it in turns to hold Squidge and say something we're worried about this morning.

SENCO starts.

SENCO: This morning, I am worried we won't get everyone into the green zone ready to start the day of learning.

DAISY: She passes to me… This morning, I am worried Paddy's going to have another one of his tantrums later.

I pass to Paddy.

"I'm worried Miss will piss me off later."

SENCO: Okay, let's stop there. We want to use language that's kind and inclusive with our worries, that doesn't make anyone go towards the red or orange zones. And I prefer the term, "outburst of emotion" to tantrum.

DAISY: Paddy passes to Gemma. Gemma throws Squidge at Yusuf and says she's bored. Yusuf doesn't understand so Ryan snatches Squidge from him. Yusuf starts crying. Ryan chucks Squidge at Tobi and says the game is stupid and he doesn't want to be in this room of retards. Yusuf starts wailing and then Tobi starts banging his head against the wall.

SENCO: What a shame. We're going to have to end the session early today because of bad behaviour choices and inappropriate language.

DAISY: I look at Paddy and he's sitting there, not bothered.

Relatable. Neither am I.

SENCO: And what's more, I won't be able to hand out Squidge to anyone this week.

DAISY: Ryan says Squidge is for babies. "We're not babies Miss."

SENCO: *(passive aggressive)* And there won't be any football.

DAISY: We're on the Daily Mile. A government-run initiative to tackle obesity in kids. We take the class on a walk every day in their morning break.

The sporty kids do three laps. The lazy ones do two. And Paddy does one. The irony isn't lost on me.

We walk, nice and slowly, round the park.

I tell him the basics of a good story. Every story has three main ingredients: beginning, middle and end. The beginning is the set-up, the middle is the problem and the end is the resolution—happy or sad.

He says he knows what I'm doing and he's not doing it. Fine. I'll tell you one.

There once was a small, sad egg. She desperately wanted to break out of her box. She wobbled and wobbled but the box wouldn't budge. She dreamt of the outside world and the kind of egg-related adventures she would get up to. She could knit an egg sweater, sit in an egg cup, meet new and exciting people she'd heard about like Mr Salt and Mrs Pepper. And then one day, the sky opened. She felt a cold breeze bounce off the top of her bald head. A human hand lifted her out of the box and she saw the world pass under her belly as she flew through the air. Then she was broken into a pan, fried and eaten.

There's a long pause as Paddy drags his feet through the autumn leaves.

Then he tells me I'm weird.

(to PADDY) Your turn.

He says he's not telling me a story, he ain't got nothing to say.

The park's a proper shithole. We've had to abort the walk twice because of reports of a flasher. Lower Sydenham is a shithole.

Paddy tells me it's not a story, but he did have a dream.

(to PADDY) Go on.

He does. He says, he had a dream a little baby was asleep on the counter. A beautiful peaceful sleeping baby. And then his mum turned round and by accident the baby started rolling off the counter and tumbling through the air but it's okay because there was a boy there to catch the baby and he was saved.

(to PADDY) That's beautiful Paddy.

And then he stops walking. His eyes glaze over. And he starts to cry.

Real sobbing. Again. Not again, I can't take it.

His shoulders start wobbling.

DAISY does the whale noises.

Fuck's sake.

—

The plumber's on call. Comes over. Comes everywhere.

After we fuck in the van, we're lying in the back on a bed of blue roll, spanners sticking into my sides from all angles and he says he's struggling a bit with childcare.

I'm worried that I know where this is going… I've got enough kids on my plate thank you. But it's not… I think he just wants someone to talk to.

He tells me he's struggling because he can't use his in-laws anymore. He can't take her there anymore. He can't take her to that house because she spends the whole time looking round it for mum.

—

I wonder what it'd be like to have a car fetish but like a real one where you get off to videos of them honking. I google "car porn" and watch a video of a Jeep jumping up and down.

Phone. Mum. Fine.

MUM: How's the new job going?

DAISY: It's shit.

MUM: Oh no, really?

DAISY: Yes.

MUM: That's a shame. Listen, I saw a fantastic documentary on Saturday that I think everyone should watch.

DAISY: I don't have a TV.

MUM: Ah well, maybe you can get it up on your laptop?

DAISY: I don't have a laptop.

MUM: Daisy, you are not the only one going through this... It's called *All the Beauty and the Bloodshed* and it's all about prescription drugs and the stigma around drug addiction and about how we should…

DAISY: I hang up.

——

Most days at school, I spend half of it outside the toilets waiting for Paddy. I think about Arthur. I try not to think about Arthur… I think about the plumber. I think about Paddy. Paddy's diet is terrible and, mixed with his general apathy for learning, he spends a lot of time on the loo so I spend a lot of time thinking. Trying not to think.

I sit next to his desk, I've even got my own kiddie chair, and we listen to most of Mr Murray's lessons. I see if there's anything I can make more accessible for Paddy.

It's fucking boring.

Geography's the worst. Mr Murray doesn't have a clue what's going on in geography. He can't actually say, "precipitation."

Maths is close second. We're doing long division and I'm resting my head on my knuckles, elbow on the desk, thinking about what lunch is on Wednesdays. It's a roast. It's a roast on Wednesdays… And a bit of dribble falls out of my mouth.

Splat. On to Paddy's desk.

And he sees. Hears the splat and sees the pool of drool on his table. He looks at me, into my eyes, and erupts with laughter. It makes me laugh too.

DAISY starts laughing, she can't contain herself.

Mr Murray looks at me and he's like "what is going on?" and we're both trying so hard to stop laughing but that makes us laugh more and eventually we have to leave. Both of us kicked out for being naughty…

One evening, I'm packing up the art supplies which are littered all over the classroom. Mr Murray lets me take art because he's also shit at it…

MR MURRAY: I'm happy to let you teach it, Daisy, but you will need to help with the clean up afterwards.

DAISY: So here I am, way past going home time stuffing pipe cleaners into the drawer that says, "Googly eyes" on it. And he says to me…

MR MURRAY: You're great with Paddy.

DAISY: Am I?

MR MURRAY: He loves you. His mam said so. Says he can't stop talking about you.

Pause.

MR MURRAY: I gave her a call about Paddy's diet for you.

DAISY: I worked it out you know. On average, he spends one hour and 37 minutes every day in the toilet. That's eight hours a week of missed lesson time.

MR MURRAY: I know.

DAISY: She gives him a choice before school, a Mars Bar or a Yorkie. She takes him into the shop and says he can choose.

MR MURRAY: I know.

Pause

MR MURRAY: She really tries you know. They haven't got it easy… I don't know if anyone told you but Paddy's younger brother passed away.

DAISY: Oh.

MR MURRAY: Yeah. When he was in Year Three. It was awful.

DAISY: What… what happened?

MR MURRAY: An accidental burn. In the bath. I won't go into the details but he was sent home from hospital with a leaflet and Paddy's parents can't read. Temperature rose. GP didn't realise the burns had got infected and by the time… it was too late.

DAISY: It really is time for me to go so I get my coat.

DAISY gets her raincoat.

And then just as I'm leaving he says…

MR MURRAY: You'd make a great teacher. A proper teacher.

DAISY: I feel this weird urge pulse up my body from my stomach to my shoulders.

MR MURRAY: Do you know why I gave you this job?

DAISY: "Because I have a nice smile?" *(to audience)* I say as I'm edging closer to the door.

MR MURRAY: No. Because when I asked you what your favourite kind of lesson would look like you said, "one where you learn to think" and when I asked you what you meant you said, "something creative, where you get to make it up." And I thought to myself "that's what makes a great teacher"—one that teaches children that they can think, not how they can think.

DAISY: I feel like I'm about to start laughing so I snort and race out of the room.

DAISY starts laughing. Then hiccupping. Her shoulders start moving uncontrollably. Up and down. Up and down.

DAISY does the whale noises and cries, gasping for air. Finally, she calms herself down, taking deep breaths, trying to count to ten.

DAISY: Why did you leave me here? In this fucking shit hole.

—

At home I try to wank. It doesn't work. I can hear the vibrator but I can't feel anything.

I call the plumber. I should probably start calling him by his name. Out of respect. Steve. Steve who says he's moving house but I should meet his kid when it's done.

Steve.

Steve doesn't answer.

He texts me, "Hey, I'm sorry for the radio silence but for the past few days I've been in a bit of a pit. It sorta hit me that you're the first person I've been with since Katy's mum. And how I said I wouldn't and how I'd only ever be there for Katy… I like you Daisy, I really do! But I can't have a proper relationship with anyone right now and I can't do phone calls I'm sorry.

And I think fuck you. It's not that deep. I just want to fuck.

And then I'm filled with this energy. It's like this mad manic energy.

DAISY starts to pace round the room.

It's like a box. I feel like the world is a box. And I'm all boxed in. I can't help you! I can't help you! I can't help you… Arthur, I can't help you.

DAISY re-enacts finding her brother—a flashback.

I can't hear… Arthur?! Arthur? Can someone help me? He's not breathing. Can someone help me get him out? Can someone help me? Arthur. CAN SOMEBODY GET HELP! PLEASE. SOMEONE. HELP!

DAISY recoils… shouting for help. She melts to the floor. Stuck in her box, she's surrounded by grief from all sides.

—

I have a Mars Bar for breakfast to see what it feels like and it's delicious.

I spend most of the day following instructions and staring at the wall. I sit next to Paddy like a giant, weirdly attractive, Year Six pupil. Geography is so boring.

Music.

Passes over me, a wave of percussion. Cymbals… cowbells… cabasas…

And then a song. Miss hands me a maraca and winks at me…

MRS WILLIAMS: *(whispers patronisingly)* The kids like it when you join in, even though you are often ever so slightly out of time…

Intro plays to Count On Me.

Bruno Mars.

They've got parts, the girls and the boys.

Daisy sings along, shaking the maraca to the beat.

GIRLS: If you ever find yourself stuck in the middle of the sea
I'll sail the world to find you

BOYS: If you ever find yourself lost in the dark and you can't see
I'll be the light to guide you

ALL: Find out what we're made of
When we are called to help our friends in need

GIRLS: You can count on me like one, two, three
I'll be there

BOYS: And I know when I need it, I can count on you like four, three, two
And you'll be there

The music keeps playing.

DAISY: And I don't know what it is. I look at Paddy and he's marching along. Swaying his round little arms. My maraca starts going out of time, like really out of time. Mrs Williams looks at me and I look at the kids.

The music warps.

I think maybe Paddy is my only friend. Paddy and Steve, Steve who doesn't want me. And my shoulders start wobbling. I know what's about to happen, so I hand the maraca to one of the children.

I'm in the corridor and I'm wheezing. Tears pouring down my face because of fucking Bruno Mars... Mr Murray's on his way to collect the kids, I see his feet coming down the stairwell.

I've got nowhere to go. I know he's going to see me. I'm boxed in, in my box of sadness and he sees me and I think he's going to say something but he doesn't.

He just hugs me.

I sob into his chest. I can feel his chin on my back. And I say, "I don't want to be a teacher. I don't want to be a teacher."

And I tell him. I don't know why I do, but I tell him. I say, "My brother died a few months ago… of an overdose. I found him in the bath and I feel like it was all my fault."

He tells me everything will be okay and I can take a moment, clean myself up and then meet us back in class and we can pretend nothing's happened.

And that's exactly what I do.

My paycheck came in on Friday so I'm looking at new cars. Nothing fancy. Just to replace my old Nelly.

Nelly is a blue Polo from the 2000s and she's dying. Why does everything die?

I drive her down to the nearest scrap yard, she grunts and pants the whole way.

I love a scrap yard. Piles and piles of shiny, rusty crap. I wish I could live here as a teeny tiny little man. And it could be my palace of brutality and armour.

Sometimes I wish I was a man. A teeny tiny one though.

The head of the scrap yard is ginger with lots of stubble and a grumbly voice. He looks at me long and hard. It feels inappropriate.

MR GRUMBLE: I'll give ya 50 squid.

DAISY: Fantastic, thanks.

And just as he's handing me over some cash, I see Paddy. His little round face poking out of his puffer jacket, kicking the dirt near a mound of metal.

(to PADDY) Paddy!

He looks my way. Asks if I'm alright Miss.

(to PADDY) Alright? I'm Daisy Wright.

He asks if that's my name, Daisy?

(to PADDY) Yeah.

He looks confused. Says he doesn't like seeing teachers outside of school because they look weird.

To be fair, I am wearing short shorts and a T-shirt so in comparison, at school, I dress like a Mormon.

(to PADDY) What're you doing here, Paddy?

He's looking for treasure, Miss.

(to PADDY, repeating him) Do I want to join?

I look around at the empty scrap yard. Grumble's gone… into the abyss. I don't really know what the protocol is. I don't really care. I know I'm not a weirdo.

I spend the afternoon learning about the intricacies of finding copper and other precious metals in Sydenham's finest scrap yard.

Paddy tells me a bit more about Ms Grimsby. Says the problem with her is… she's a dumb bitch.

MS GRIMSBY: Don't you want more for yourself Paddy? Don't you think your dad does too?

DAISY: He can make loads of money round the yard. Says he used to go with his dad but now he can be trusted to go by himself and still get the good stuff. Because he's the oldest.

My dad's a king. And Ms Grimsby's a dumb bitch.

(to PADDY) You can be king of the yard, Paddy, if you want to be. Or you could start a pet shop. You can do anything you set your mind to.

Then how come I never get Squidge?

(to PADDY) You don't need Squidge, Paddy.

He tells me everyone needs Squidge.

(to PADDY) Just keep reading about animals and then come here on the weekends and you can decide later.

He says his dad wants him to skip school. Start earning a proper living. But he'll keep reading with me. He'll read about animals with me.

And then it feels like the air gets thicker and it's hard to breathe.

(aside) I can't help you.

Are you okay, Miss?

(to PADDY) I better head back, Paddy.

He asks if I've got big plans this evening? You got a hot date Miss?

DAISY manages a laugh.

On my way out of the scrap yard, Grumble stops me.

MR GRUMBLE: You want to be careful love, not to wear your sadness like a badge.

DAISY: Excuse me?

MR GRUMBLE: If you wear your sadness like a badge it'll become your identity and you won't be able to get rid of it. Listen to your heart, be open and fight it off. You've got to fight off the sadness.

DAISY: An absolutely absurd piece of advice to come from Grumble, I think, as I dodge him and leave through the gates of the yard.

—

Mum decides to take me to yoga. I meet her outside a crusty church hall at half past six.

MUM: I'm okay. Given the circumstances.

DAISY: The yoga teacher has a pot belly and I imagine her after class, dipping Wotsits into a banana milkshake.

YOGA TEACHER: Welcome to neurogenic yoga, a form of yoga that unlocks tension and trauma.

DAISY: She locks the door. Fuck.

I scowl at Mum but she's sitting cross-legged on her mat with her eyes closed.

The teacher gets on her back and sticks her pelvis in the air. Everyone, except me, does the same.

YOGA TEACHER: Breath in… and start to shake.

DAISY: The room starts to wobble. Mum looks like the Jeep from porn hub.

MUM: Come on, Daisy, give it a go.

DAISY: Tears start rolling down her face, splattering onto the mat. Someone at the back starts groaning.

DAISY does a high-pitched groaning sound.

I feel like I'm in some kind of a voodoo prayer room, like Mum's going to burst into flames and little baby zombies are going to burst out of the teacher's pot belly.

Groaning.

I roll up my prayer mat and take it to the door. Dodge the bodies shaking left, right and centre.

MUM: Daisy, come back.

DAISY: She's following me. We're by the door, her wet face and glossy eyes up close like a portal to the zombie apocalypse.

MUM: Daisy, it's good to feel sadness.

DAISY: I'm desperately tampering with the lock trying to get out.

MUM: Daisy, try it. Think of something really sad. It's okay to cry.

DAISY: I think of a cat being squished by a lorry. But the thought of those big wheels just makes me horny.

—

I'm on my sofa. I spend my life here. Outside the male kiddie toilets and here, sinking into my sofa.

She reaches for her phone.

I google lizard jokes about reptile disfunction. Decide to look Steve up on Facebook. I have his surname from the text the council sent me when I had the leak, "Steve Ridley is on the way."

Steve. Ridley. There are loads of them. I don't know why I haven't done this before. Ah that's him. Profile picture at work with a can of WD-40. Fit. He's shown me that before. 21st August. That's when we met. I remember because it was the day after the funeral.

Oof. One of the whole family, they're dressed up for Halloween. Steve, baby, baby Muma. Ketchup, mustard, mayo. That is sad.

I don't know how she died but he said it was a few days after Katy was born.

Oh God, she's tagged in this one. It's a selfie of them together. I go to click on her. I'm not sure I can do it—look at a dead person's Facebook, they're awful. I'm surprised he hasn't got rid of it...

Fuck it. Nothing to lose. I click on her. Cute. Looks a bit like me really, bit more like a chipmunk. Nice smile.

I scroll down for all those RIP messages people put on their profiles. There are none.

Click on her profile picture. The two of them at home in May.

So she's only been dead for five months?! And that's if she died straight after this photo.

Unless…

She's not dead.

She's definitely alive. Find her LinkedIn. TikTok. Twitter.

I call him. He answers. I say I found his Facebook and there's some stuff which doesn't quite add up.

He says that's odd because he doesn't have Facebook which I say is odd because I'm staring at it…

I hang up.

My mind is whirling. I am in shock. I refresh his profile but it says content unavailable.

Pause.

I think about the stories he told me. His life as a single dad. About her teeny tiny birthday cake, "just for the two of us". How hard it was to fix the toilet and watch her have no one to play with. The image I have, the image of baby looking round the house for Mum!

Whatever. It was just a fuck.

Pause.

Actually it's a bit hurtful. I mean. That's a bit fucked up. That's fucked up to pretend someone's dead. Because some people really do die. And she's not dead. And I'm not dead. Which means we're both alive.

I lie on the floor staring at the ceiling for a long time.

When I get up, it's 10pm. I call my mum. I don't know why, but it's ringing and I'm waiting for her to answer so I guess that's what I'm doing.

MUM: Hi, darling.

DAISY: It's me.

MUM: Are you doing okay?

DAISY: There's a long pause because… because…

(to MUM) I'm not okay.

Then I think she's going to say something irrelevant but she doesn't. She just listens. Listens to the silence.

So I fill it.

(to MUM) I'm not okay, Mum. I'm swimming in grief and I thought I had someone to share it with but I don't because they made it all up. I feel like I've got the world on my shoulders even though I know I don't. I'm only paid £13.15 an hour and that's not enough to carry the world on your shoulders. But I do, I feel like I'm carrying it because the little boy that I teach he needs me to read and without me he won't read and I feel like I can't take that on. And to take it on I've been pretending that I don't care.

About anything.

Because if I don't care then nothing can hurt me. And I can carry Paddy because it doesn't matter if he falls off, because nothing matters.

But the truth is, it does matter. To me. I do care.

I care about Paddy and I care that Arthur's dead and nothing will bring him back and he was my brother, my actual brother. And I feel like it's all my fault. I care that so much bad stuff happens and that there are bad people that make it even worse.

This world is full of drug addicts and grief and people that are fucked up in the head. And I don't understand why we have to pretend that everything smells like fucking roses when it stinks of fish. It stinks of fish.

And then she says,

MUM: Your dad and I had kippers this morning...

Pause.

Anyway darling, I hear what you're saying. The world is full of drug addicts and bad people but the thing that matters more than anything is what you just said, that you care. Because that's what we all have to decide. Do we care enough to power on through the grief? Despite the grief. And choose love. It's not your fault what happened to Arthur. It is not your fault.

DAISY: I'm about to hang up but then I hear myself say, "Mum? Can we watch that documentary together? The one about prescription drugs?"

MUM: I'll call you tomorrow.

DAISY: And I know that she will.

It's 4pm and the kids have gone home and I'm making a cup of tea in the staff room.

I hate the staffroom. Teachers are so used to talking to a classroom full of kids they don't know how to turn the volume down.

And the topics of conversation are dull and boring. Google maps. Reception. Keir Starmer. Tenerife. Year Six. Year Three. Parking. Rishi Sunak. Year Two. The cost of living. Keir Starmer.

Ms Grimsby is tearing the ear off anyone who will listen. I've tucked myself away in the corner on one of those fabric chairs that remind me of nits because the nurse at my primary school wouldn't let us sit on them, in case we had nits. She said they'd jump off our heads and live in the chairs. She didn't want her chairs to get nits.

MS GRIMSBY: I know. Absolute pain that child. Honestly. I know he's been abused but, my God, his behaviour… God forbid he's with me next year. It's maddening how one child can affect the whole class. Change the dynamic completely, disrupt everything… I had this a couple of years ago. Paddy Connors. Nightmare. You're his 1:1 aren't you?

DAISY looks over her shoulder at the wall.

DAISY: Is she talking to me?

DAISY nods.

(to MS GRIMSBY) Yeah.

MS GRIMSBY: Ha! That must be a challenge. How are you coping? I'd give you until Christmas…

DAISY: We've increased his reading age by a year in less than two months.

MS GRIMSBY: Oh wow. How did you manage that? Mars Bars?

Pause.

DAISY: I feel angry. I don't know why. But it stops me thinking before I speak.

(to MS GRIMSBY) No. He wants to learn.

There's a pause and her lip curls but before she can say anything, I can't help myself…

(to MS GRIMSBY) It's his lack of confidence that stops him wanting to learn not his ability. Something awful happened to him in Year Three but it wasn't his fault and he was depressed but the teacher he had just sat him at the back of the classroom, facing the back wall. He was completely isolated and left to his own

devices. So since then, his confidence in education and in himself has been destroyed as well as having to deal with depression and grief at a very young age. I haven't had to use Mars Bars to get him to read, I just talk to him about things he likes doing and show him that he can do them if he tries and then I tell him that he's brave for even trying. Because I care.

And then I stand up from the chair, spilling my tea in the process, and walk right out of the staffroom leaving my nits behind me.

I think to myself, good point well made. That's what my mum would say.

—

Paddy and I read about snakes. Paddy has an outburst of emotion. Paddy learns how to add two-digit numbers.

Paddy sits on the loo… He gets extra toilet allowance because Mr Murray tells me he's got contact dermatitis.

MR MURRAY: Nothing to worry about—just caused from excessive wiping. But if he needs extra time in the bathroom, you can let him have it.

DAISY: Snakes. Numbers. Toilet. Toilet. Numbers. Snakes. Snakes. Reptiles. Animals.

Fire alarm.

I stick by Paddy and he grips my sleeve. I think the noise of the alarm is unsettling him.

(whispers to PADDY) Paddy… What do you call a lizard that makes jokes?

It's amazing the fire drill. Everyone excited and self-important. Except the kids. They drag their heels as they shuffle out into the cold without an ounce of anticipation at the possibility of fire!

Outside in the prison yard, I see Ms Grimsby muttering away to Mr Murray. She keeps looking over to me as she talks which makes me think she's talking about me. Bitch. I stare at her.

And she's jabbering away, using her finger to point at me. Bitch. So I let go of Paddy and I march over there.

(to MS GRIMSBY) Is there something you'd like to say to me?

Mr Murray gestures with his hand that I should take it easy...

(to MR MURRAY) Calm down? How'd you expect me to calm down? This woman is a bitch and she shouldn't be a teacher.

The whole school is out on the playground and the whole school is being quiet because it's a fire drill so the whole school hears me call Ms Grimsby a bitch.

Silence.

(to MR MURRAY) I'm sorry but I'm not sorry. I don't know what she's saying to you, but I think she should take some responsibility for her actions. If she's rude about people in the staffroom, then she can expect to face the consequences. It's not okay not to care. People's lives are at stake. And if you don't care then you're a bad teacher and I'll tell you that to your face.

(to MS GRIMSBY) You're a bad teacher.

I feel a tugging at my arm, and I look down and it's Paddy. He's saying something. He's saying, "It's a stand-up chameleon, Miss. A lizard that makes jokes. We can go back inside now Miss. Look."

I look up and the younger years are starting to make their way back into the building.

It's not worth it Miss.

He grabs me by the hand and drags me inside. And then it's the weekend.

—

I blocked the plumber which means I'm alone again. All by myself. But it's quiet. It's peaceful. No more fires.

On Sunday night, Mr Murray calls me. For once I'm not sitting on my sofa but cooking. Ratatouille. It looks disgusting and I can't believe I'm going to eat it.

MR MURRAY: Daisy. How are you?

DAISY: I'm good.

MR MURRAY: Did you have a nice weekend?

DAISY: Yeah.

MR MURRAY: Get some rest?

DAISY: Mmhmm.

MR MURRAY: Listen, I have to say above everything, thank you for all your hard work with Paddy. We've seen a huge improvement and I want you to know that I'm very grateful and know his family are also.

DAISY tries the ratatouille and burns herself.

DAISY: Ow. Fuck.

MR MURRAY: Sorry?

DAISY: Nothing, sorry.

MR MURRAY: Look. Daisy. Ms Grimsby's not someone to make an enemy of. She's made a complaint against you and they're going to ask you to leave tomorrow. I wanted to tell you before you have your meeting. I tried to fight for you, I really did, but calling her a bitch in front of the kids… It's, well it's a fireable offence. Especially because you haven't apologised…

DAISY: Got it. No problem, Andy. Thanks for letting me know.

She hangs up.

—

DAISY mimes squidging the air into Squidge.

This morning, I am worried the world stinks of fish.

This morning, I'm worried about Paddy.

This morning, I am worried I'll lose my job.

I go in early for the Special Education Needs session anyway.

SENCO is late so I take the session and we play football.

Ryan has to sit out because he starts shouting inappropriate and highly offensive insults at his teammates when the other team scores a goal.

We're sitting in a circle to round up the session and I ask the kids to close their eyes. I ask them to imagine a friend and to tell that friend something that they love about them.

Then I ask them to imagine that they're their friend. What would they say they love about you.

Ryan starts crying. Says he's just got something in his eye, Miss.

(to the kids) And I know that it's for babies but sometimes it's nice to have things babies have so I'm going to hand out Squidge.

DAISY mimes collecting Squidge from the top of her head and moulding him into a little box shape in the palm of her hand.

I'm going to give Squidge to Paddy today. Because I saw him about to give up when Ryan got sent off. But he didn't.

Ryan says surely that means he should get Squidge.

No, it's going to Paddy. What colour would you like Squidge to be Paddy?

He says he wants it to be grey.

She mimes painting it grey with some paint from inside a tiny imaginary cupboard.

Amazing. Any glitter?

He says, no thanks, Miss.

She mimes popping it onto PADDY's head.

I take him back to class before I have to go to the headmaster's office for my meeting.

On our way up the stairs, he says something to me. He says, "Miss, can I add something to Squidge please?"

(to PADDY) Sure.

Can you put, "R.I.P. Finny" on him?

She takes Squidge off the top of his head and mimes painting the little letters onto it.

There.

She places Squidge back on his head and smiles.

—

He strolls into class, letting the door close behind him. I watch him find his desk through the rectangular window in the classroom door. And then I make my way to the headmaster's office.

I'm early so I sit next to Ryan on the kiddie bench outside the office. And I think why don't they make anything for fucking adults in this place?

I realise I'm still holding the little paint brush between my index finger and my thumb. So I get my own Squidge and write, "Arthur." In teeny tiny little letters on him.

DAISY flicks away the paint brush. She hears the kids singing Bruno Mars somewhere in the school.

GIRLS: You can count on me like one, two, three
I'll be there

BOYS: And I know when I need it
I can count on you like four, three, two
And you'll be there

DAISY: I decide that I'm not going to give up this job. I'm going to go in there and I'm going to fight for it. I'll start by saying that I'm sorry, even though I'm not, because I will not lose this job. I will not give up. I will not give up.

Pause.

I ask Ryan why he's sat here. How did you manage to get in trouble in the five minutes you've been back to class?

He says he didn't Miss, he just prefers it out here than in the classroom, Miss. You?

I was rude to Miss Grimsby.

Oh that's rough, Miss… she's a right bitch!

Daisy smiles.

BLACKOUT.

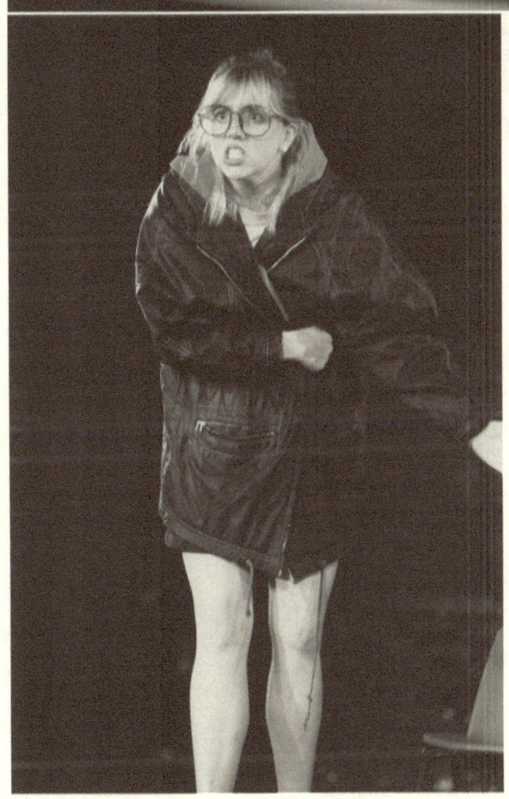

SUPPORT NUMBERS

Actors' Benevolent Fund
Helpline: 020 7836 3330
Website: https://www.actorsbenevolentfund.co.uk

Al-Anon Family Groups
Helpline: 0800 0086 811
Website: https://www.al-anonuk.org.uk

Ashton Jazz Academy for Young People
Website: https://www.ashdonjazzacademy.org.uk/

Childline
Helpline: 0800 1111
Website: https://www.childline.org.uk

Cruse Bereavement Care
Helpline: 0808 808 1677
Website: https://www.cruse.org.uk

Equity Charitable Trust
Website: https://www.equitycharitabletrust.org.uk

National Education Union
Helpline: 0345 811 8111
Website: https://neu.org.uk

Pavee Point
Helpline: 01 878 0255
Website: https://www.paveepoint.ie

Support for Key Workers
Helpline: 0800 056 6742
Website: https://www.keyworker.support

Writers' Guild of Great Britain
Helpline: 020 7833 0777
Website: https://www.writersguild.org.uk

Winston's Wish
Helpline: 08088 020 021
Website: https://www.winstonswish.org

Young Minds
Helpline: 0808 802 5544
Website: https://www.youngminds.org.uk

ALSO AVAILABLE FROM SALAMANDER STREET

All Salamander Street plays can be bought in bulk at a discount for performance or study. Contact info@salamanderstreet.com to enquire about performance licenses.

EAT THE RICH (but maybe not me mates x)
by Jade Franks
ISBN: 9781068233449

Witty, provocative and utterly current—a bold exploration of class, privilege and power from one of the UK's most exciting new playwrights.

THE OLIVE BOY
by Ollie Maddigan
ISBN: 9781068233487

Based on his real life story, Ollie Maddigan's Offie-winning solo show introduces The Olive Boy. Forced to change schools and move in with a man he barely knows, The Olive Boy is attempting to stay sane and finally get a real girlfriend.

CARA AND KELLY ARE BEST FRIENDS FOREVER FOR LIFE by Mojola Akinyemi
ISBN: 9781068233418

A darkly comic two-hander that exposes the nastiest sides of teenage girlhood.

ALGORITHMS
by Sadie Clark

ISBN: 9781738429394

A bisexual Bridget Jones for the online generation, this tragicomic solo show, and its lovably hapless heroine, is for anyone who's ever felt like they were too much and not enough at the same time.

WORMHOLES by Emily Jupp

ISBN: 9781068696206

A gripping solo play about coercive control, domestic abuse and how the mind finds a way to escape.

www.salamanderstreet.com

www.ingramcontent.com/pod-product-compliance
Lightning Source LLC
La Vergne TN
LVHW050946080826
845145LV00004B/1425